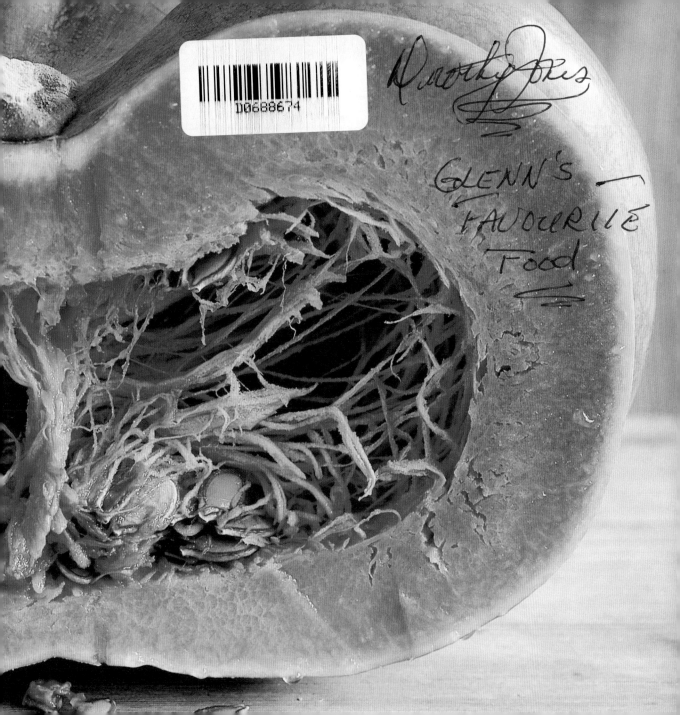

Dorothy Jones

GLENN'S
FAVOURITE
FOOD

cooking with **pumpkins**
and squash

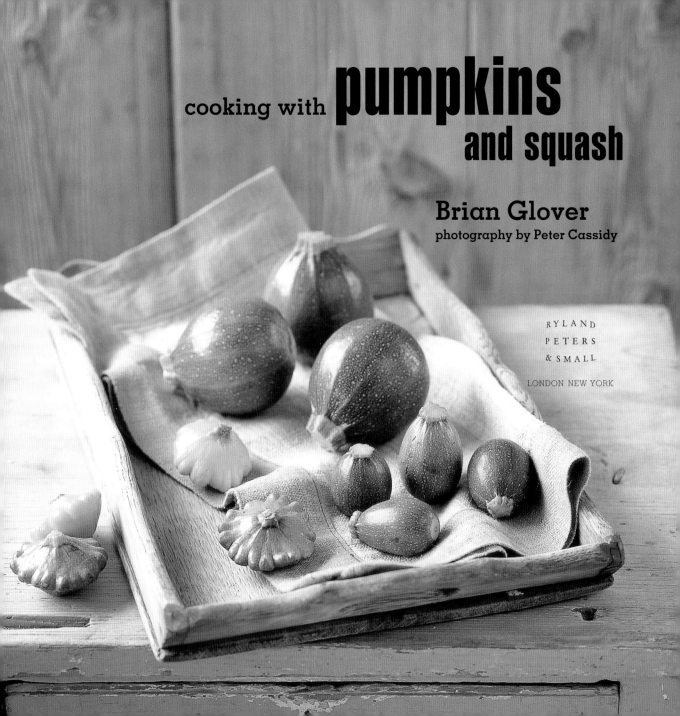

cooking with **pumpkins**
and squash

Brian Glover

photography by Peter Cassidy

RYLAND
PETERS
& SMALL

LONDON NEW YORK

Dedication

To my mother, who sowed the seed of a lifelong love of growing plants.

Design and photographic art direction
Steve Painter
Commissioning Editor Julia Charles
Production Controller Gemma John
Art Director Leslie Harrington
Publishing Director Alison Starling

Food Stylist Linda Tubby
Prop Stylist Roisin Nield
Index Hilary Bird

Author's acknowledgments
Thank you to the team at Ryland, Peters & Small, especially Julia Charles and Steve Painter, plus Linda Tubby and Peter Cassidy for the beautiful photography.

First published in the United States in 2008 by Ryland Peters & Small Inc.
519 Broadway
5th Floor
New York, NY 10012
www.rylandpeters.com

Text © Brian Glover 2008
Design and photographs
© Ryland Peters & Small 2008

10 9 8 7 6 5 4 3 2

Printed in China

Library of Congress Cataloging-in-Publication Data

Glover, Brian, 1958-
  Cooking with pumpkins and squash / Brian Glover ; photography by Peter Cassidy.
    p. cm.
  Includes index.
  ISBN 978-1-84597-708-5
  1. Cookery (Squash) 2. Cookery (Pumpkin) I. Title.
  TX803.S67G56 2008
  641.6'562--dc22

2008007925

Notes
• All herbs used in these recipes are fresh unless specified as dried.
• All spoon measurements are level unless otherwise specified.
• Ovens should be preheated to the specified temperatures. All ovens work slightly differently. We suggest you consult the maker's handbook for any special instructions, particularly if you are using a fan-assisted oven, as you may need to adjust temperatures accordingly.
• To sterilize jars, wash well in soapy water, rinse thoroughly, then boil in plenty of water for 10 minutes. They should be filled as soon as they are dry, and still hot. For further information on preserving visit: http://hgic.clemson.edu/food.htm

contents

introduction

There are myriad varieties of squash. They range from tiny, finger-sized zucchini, still sporting their crystalline flowers, to huge, heavyweight pumpkins that reach the weight of a grown man. Some squash have beautiful orange and red skins, others come in bizarre, often comical shapes or with knobbly eruptions. They all belong to the Curcurbitaceae family, which also includes cucumbers, melons, and gourds. Some varieties of winter squash, such as the fabled Sucrine du Berry, betray the family connection, being almost as sweet as honeydew melon.

Squashes are an amazingly versatile ingredient for the venturesome cook. Delicate summer squash, such as young zucchini, need nothing more than gentle cooking and a handful of chopped summer herbs such as chervil, mint, chives, or basil to make the best of simple "sauces" for pasta. Larger zucchini can be grilled and tossed into salads, sliced into omelets and risotto, grated to make fritters and cakes or left whole to stuff and bake. Even the delicate yellow blossoms of the zucchini are delicious when battered and deep-fried.

Winter squash are hardy and can take more robust treatment. Roasting or pan-frying concentrates their flavor to a sweet, chestnutty richness. They make a great base for soups and stews, but are also wonderful stirred into pasta or rice dishes, or layered and baked in creamy gratins.

Some flavors stand out as having a real affinity with squashes and pumpkins of all shapes and sizes: their nutty sweetness works well with salty tastes such as goat cheese, feta, and olives. For seasoning try the muskiness of sage, cumin, or nutmeg, or the spicy heat of chile. Mostly, we think of savory flavors when we cook with squash, but it picks up the sweetness of sugar too. Used in pies, tarts, puddings, and preserves, it cries out for warm spices such as cinnamon and ginger as well a hint of citrus sharpness and the smooth richness of butter and cream.

The many varieties of squash

Not only do squash come in many shapes and sizes, they also come with all sorts of names. To add to the confusion, some varieties are called more than one thing. For example, Red Kuri or Uchiki Kuri squash are sometimes known as just plain Kuri or even Red Onion. So, from all this confusing variety, how do we choose what to cook and eat? For the cook, the big division is between summer and winter squash.

Summer squash have soft, edible skins, easily scraped with a thumbnail, and creamy white flesh—they are best eaten soon after harvesting. When they are young you can eat the whole thing, skins, seeds, and all. The best-known summer squash is the zucchini. **Zucchini** can be light or dark green, striped, or even a beautiful buttery yellow. There are round zucchinis too and these are best eaten when they are no bigger than a tennis ball. You can also eat the delicate blossoms and the young leaves. In Italian markets you will often see baby zucchini still with their blossom attached. You can coat the blossoms in a light batter and deep-fry them, stuff them or simply serve them torn into a salad. Other summer squashes to look out for are the small and very cute, scallop-edged **Pattypans** and **Custard Pie** squashes. Some would describe **Marrows** as just overgrown zucchini. Their size makes them ideal for stuffing and baking whole.

Winter squash (including pumpkins) have tough, hard skins, which aren't usually eaten and yellow-orange flesh; many of them can be stored for months in a cool, frost-free place. The seeds have to be removed from winter squash, though they can be cleaned and lightly roasted to make a delicious snack. The Austrians also use pumpkin seeds to produce a deep-flavored, slightly smoky cooking oil. **Butternut** is undoubtedly the most popular winter squash and no wonder. It tastes deliciously sweet and nutty when roasted or pan-fried and it is not so dry-fleshed or starchy as some varieties. You can use it for almost all the savory recipes in this book, but there is a wealth of other varieties, especially at farmers' markets, farm shops and country markets, so do shop around and experiment.

Red Kuri squash are beautifully colored, small to medium-sized squash with an excellent savory flavor and because of their size they are perfect for roasting whole or halved or used as an edible "bowl" for a stew or soup. Japanese varieties such as **Kabocha** and **Hokkaido**, as well as **Turk's Cap** and **Crown Prince**, are medium-sized squash with a long shelf life and are good all-rounders in the kitchen. Kabocha and Crown Prince have a drier, starchier flesh that roasts or pan fries to a wonderful chestnutty texture; these varieties are good for mashes, purées and gnocchi. Small varieties such as **Sweet Dumpling**, **Acorn**, **Golden Nugget**, and **Sugar Loaf** are excellent for roasting whole, either stuffed or plain. Also look out for the medium-sized, striped **Delicata** squash, which has a taste reminiscent of sweet potato.

Most French and Italian varieties are superb for cooking, which is no surprise as that's what they have been bred for. Try the bizarrely tuba-shaped **Tromba d'Albenga**, the sweet **Sucrine du Berry**, or the **Jaspée de Vendée** (all excellent for pies). The French variety **Musque de Provence** is beautiful as well as good to eat. If you don't want to buy a whole, huge pumpkin, West Indian, Caribbean, and Greek stores often sell wedges of the large, tan-colored **Calabaza pumpkin**. This again is a good all-rounder in the kitchen with a moist flesh but a lovely flavor.

Halfway between a summer and a winter squash, the **Spaghetti squash** is something of an oddity. Once cooked, the pale creamy flesh can be removed in thin strands resembling spaghetti pasta. An orange-fleshed variety delights in the name **Hasta la Pasta!** Because of the likeness to pasta it is often served tossed with tomato sauce, just like pasta, but its light flavor and texture is also excellent in a salad (dress it while still warm in a mustardy vinaigrette) or baked in a rich, creamy gratin.

Oddly enough, one of the few varieties that isn't that good to eat is the most familiar—the red-orange **Halloween** or **Cinderella pumpkin (Rouge Vif d'Etampes)**. It's really an ornamental pumpkin and the flesh tends to be fibrous and watery. You can use it to make a base for puréed soups, but it's really best kept for jack o' lanterns.

light bites

zucchini & ricotta fritters with tomato avocado salsa

3 zucchini (about 10–12 oz.)

8 oz. ricotta cheese

2 large eggs, separated

¾ cup all-purpose flour

3–5 tablespoons milk

4 scallions, thinly sliced

3 tablespoons mixed chopped herbs, such as parsley, dill, mint, and cilantro

½ teaspoon cream of tartar

sea salt and freshly ground black pepper

olive or safflower oil, for sautéing

for the salsa

1 large ripe (but not soft) avocado

8 oz. ripe tomatoes, deseeded and diced

1 large kiwi fruit, peeled and diced

grated zest and freshly squeezed juice of 1 unwaxed lime, plus extra juice to taste

1 medium red or green chile, seeded and finely chopped

1 small red onion, finely chopped

2 tablespoons mixed chopped mint and cilantro leaves

roasted ground cumin and superfine sugar, to taste

1 teaspoon Thai fish sauce (optional)

Makes 18–20 small fritters

These green-flecked little fritters seem to me the essence of summer cooking—herby, fresh-tasting, and quick to cook. You don't have to serve the fritters with the tomato salsa, though I love the contrast of the hot, crisp fritter with the cool, chile-spiked fruity salsa—you could serve them as they are with lemon wedges and a little melted butter.

Trim the ends from the zucchini, then grate coarsely. Toss with 1 teaspoon salt and put in a colander to drain for 45 minutes. Rinse, then squeeze dry with your hands or in a dry, clean kitchen towel.

Meanwhile, make the salsa. Peel and pit the avocado then chop into small dice. Put it in a non-reactive bowl with the tomatoes, kiwi, lime zest, chile, red onion, and herbs. Add a pinch of cumin and fish sauce (if using) with the lime juice. Toss to mix thoroughly, then let stand while you make the fritters.

In a bowl, beat together the ricotta with the eggs yolks, flour, and 3 tablespoons milk to make a thick batter. Fold in the zucchini, scallions, and chopped herbs. Season with black pepper and a little extra salt. Add the extra milk only if the mixture seems too stiff. Whisk the egg whites and cream of tartar in a separate, grease-free bowl until stiff, then fold into the flour mixture to make a light batter.

In a large, non-stick skillet, heat 3–4 tablespoons oil over medium heat then add spoonfuls of the batter to make little pancakes, about 3 inches across. Sauté for about 4–5 minutes on each side until browned and set. Keep the batches warm in a low oven as you make all the fritters, adding extra oil to the pan as necessary.

Taste the salsa and add salt, pepper, sugar, more cumin, and/or lime juice to taste, then serve with the hot fritters.

spiced squash & feta phyllo pastries

3 tablespoons olive oil

¼ teaspoon dried hot pepper flakes

1 lb. prepared squash, such as Butternut, cut into ½-inch dice

6 scallions, thinly sliced

1 rounded teaspoon cumin seeds, lightly crushed

1 garlic clove, finely chopped

2 tablespoons each finely chopped flatleaf parsley and dill

6–7 oz. feta cheese, diced

freshly squeezed lemon juice, to taste

8 sheets of phyllo pastry, thawed if frozen

6 tablespoons unsalted butter, melted

2 tablespoons sesame seeds

sea salt and freshly ground black pepper

Makes 24 small pastries

There is something about the sweet taste of pan-fried or roasted squash that works particularly well with the salty taste of fresh feta cheese. Add a bite of hot pepper flakes and a crisp wrapping of buttery phyllo pastry and you have an ideal appetizer to serve with drinks. These little parcels also make great picnic food. Serve them warm with a cool cucumber and yogurt salad. Just stir chopped, salted, and drained cucumber, crushed garlic and plenty of chopped fresh mint into Greek yogurt.

Make the filling first. Heat the oil in a large skillet over medium heat. Add the hot pepper flakes and squash and sauté gently, stirring every now and then, until the squash is tender and lightly browned, about 7–8 minutes. Add the onions, cumin, and garlic, then sauté gently for another 2–3 minutes. Allow to cool, then mix in a bowl with the herbs and feta. Season to taste with lemon juice, salt, and pepper.

Preheat the oven to 375°F. Lightly grease one or two large baking sheets. Working with one sheet of phyllo at a time (and keeping the remainder covered to prevent it drying out), cut each sheet lengthways into three strips.

Brush each strip with a little melted butter. Put a heaped tablespoon of filling at one end of each strip, then fold up the pastry to enclose the filling in a triangle. Continue to fold up the strip of pastry to make a multi-layered triangle. Place each triangle on a prepared baking sheet as you finish it and continue until all the phyllo and filling has been used. Brush the top of each pastry with a little melted butter, sprinkle with a few sesame seeds, then bake in the preheated oven for 20–25 minutes until crisp and golden brown.

roasted flat mushrooms with spiced squash & chickpea stuffing

1 small squash (about 2 lbs.), peeled, seeded and diced

5–6 tablespoons olive oil

a small bunch of thyme

¼ teaspoon dried hot pepper flakes

1 garlic clove, chopped

1 x 14-oz. can chickpeas, drained

½–1 teaspoon ground toasted cumin seeds

freshly squeezed lemon juice, to taste

1–2 tablespoons chopped flatleaf parsley

1–2 tablespoons crème fraîche or heavy cream (optional)

8 large, flat portobello mushrooms, stalks removed

¼ cup toasted pumpkin seeds

sea salt and freshly ground black pepper

for the sauce

1 garlic clove

a pinch of coarse sea salt

3–4 tablespoons tahini

freshly squeezed lemon juice, to taste

4–5 tablespoons plain yogurt

1 tablespoon chopped mint

Serves 4

This is good enough to serve as a meat-free main when entertaining friends (or use smaller mushrooms and serve as an appetizer), but also delicious as a family dinner dish, as it is full of warm, comforting flavors. Serve with rice pilaf and a spinach salad. Use a squash with a dryish, chestnutty flesh such as Kabocha or Burgess Buttercup.

Preheat the oven to 425°F. Toss the squash with 3 tablespoons of the oil, 1 teaspoon chopped thyme, the hot pepper flakes, and garlic. Season and put on a baking sheet. Cover with foil and cook in the preheated oven for about 30 minutes until tender, then uncover and cook for a further 10 minutes. Let cool and put in a food processor with the chickpeas. Whizz to make a rough purée. Season to taste with salt, pepper, cumin, and lemon juice, then stir in the parsley. If the purée is very dry, add the crème fraîche or a little water.

Meanwhile, put the mushrooms, gill-side uppermost, on an oiled baking sheet. Season and sprinkle with a few thyme leaves. Drizzle with the remaining oil and a good squeeze of lemon juice. Roast, uncovered, in the preheated oven for 15 minutes until just cooked. Remove from the oven and reduce the heat to 375°F.

Distribute the stuffing between the mushrooms. Scatter with the pumpkin seeds and a few thyme sprigs. Spoon over a little of the mushroom cooking juices, then return them to the oven for 10 minutes to heat through. To make the sauce, mash the garlic with the salt in a bowl, then gradually work in 3 tablespoons tahini, followed by 1 tablespoon lemon juice. When smooth, gradually work in the yogurt, then taste and add more lemon juice and/or tahini as necessary. Stir in the mint and serve with the mushrooms.

squash & sage frittata

¼ cup olive oil

2 large sweet onions, halved and thinly sliced

¼ teaspoon dried hot pepper flakes (or more to taste), crushed

2 garlic cloves, peeled and halved

1 Butternut squash (about 1½ lbs.) peeled, seeded, and diced

1 tablespoon finely shredded sage leaves

8 large eggs

2–3 tablespoons chopped flatleaf parsley

1 tablespoon butter

5 oz. firm goat cheese, cubed

sea salt and freshly ground black pepper

Serves 4 or cuts into 24–30 pieces for an appetizer

There is something about the musty sharpness of sage that works so well with the sweetness of caramelized squash. This frittata is a very adaptable dish—cut into wedges and served with a peppery green salad, it makes a great lunch. Cut into much smaller, bite-size pieces, it works well as a appetizer with drinks. Stuffed into a hollowed-out crusty loaf and drizzled with extra virgin olive oil, it's suitable for even the most stylish of picnics.

In a medium-large skillet with a lid, heat the oil over medium heat. Add the onions and 2 good pinches of salt. Stir, then cover and reduce the heat to low. Cook very gently, stirring occasionally, until the onions are meltingly soft and golden yellow, about 20 minutes.

Raise the heat slightly and add the hot pepper flakes, garlic, and squash. Stir to cover in the oily onions and cook gently, stirring frequently, until the squash is just tender, about 10 minutes. Discard the garlic. Sauté the squash a little more until it starts to brown, then stir in the sage and cook for a few more minutes. Let it cool slightly.

In a bowl, whisk the eggs and beat in the parsley, then stir in the cooked squash and onions. Season with a little salt and black pepper. Put the skillet back over medium heat and preheat the broiler to medium. Add the butter to the skillet, and as it foams, pour in the egg and squash mixture and use a spatula to level it. Scatter the goat cheese evenly over the top. Cook for about 5–6 minutes until the underside is golden brown and set. Put the frittata under the preheated broiler and cook until it is evenly browned, slightly puffed up and the egg is fully set. Serve warm or at room temperature.

zucchini, cheese, & herb muffins

2 tablespoons olive oil

6 oz. small zucchini, topped, tailed and very thinly sliced into roundels or finely diced

2 scallions, thinly sliced

1 red chile, seeded and finely chopped

1½ teaspoons chopped thyme, plus 18 small sprigs

1¼ cups all-purpose flour

⅓ cup fine yellow cornmeal or organic kamut* flour

2 teaspoons baking powder

½ teaspoon baking soda

1 teaspoon superfine sugar

1 cup freshly grated Parmesan cheese

½ teaspoon paprika

1 large egg, beaten with ⅔ cup sour cream and ¼ cup milk

4 tablespoons butter, melted and cooled, or vegetable oil

5 oz. firm goat cheese or feta cheese, cut into small cubes

sea salt and freshly ground black pepper

an 18-hole muffin pan, lined with paper cases

Makes 18 muffins or 30 mini muffins

*Kamut is an ancient wheat related to the durum variety. The flour is unrefined and often used in modern breadmaking.

These savory muffins are just right for a lazy brunch or as an accompaniment to a bowl of soup. Made small, they are ideal to pass around with drinks at a party. They are best eaten freshly made and still warm, but can be reheated for a few minutes in a low oven. These look very pretty made with small, finger-length zucchini, especially if you use a mixture of green and yellow.

Preheat the oven to 400°F. Heat the oil in a small skillet over medium heat, then add the zucchini, onions, and chile. Add a pinch of salt and cook very gently for 3–4 minutes until the zucchini have lost their raw look, but still retain a crispness. They should not brown. Stir in the chopped thyme and let cool.

Sift the flour, cornmeal, baking powder, baking soda, and sugar into a bowl and stir in ¾ teaspoon salt, a little black pepper, two-thirds of the Parmesan and the paprika. Rapidly mix the beaten egg mixture and the melted butter into the dry ingredients (do not overmix), then stir in the zucchini mixture and goat cheese.

Spoon the mixture into the lined muffin pan. Sprinkle each muffin with the remaining Parmesan and top with a thyme sprig. Bake in the preheated oven for 20–25 minutes—they should just spring back to a light touch. Serve warm.

Note: If you do want to make smaller muffins, line a 30–36-hole mini-muffin pan with small paper cases, fill with the mixture and reduce the baking time to 15–20 minutes. Be careful not to overbake them.

roasted squash wedges with pumpkin seed pesto

1 medium-sized winter squash or 2 smaller ones, such as Butternut or Red Kuri, unpeeled

extra virgin olive oil, to drizzle

a few sage leaves

for the pesto

3 tablespoons pumpkin seeds

1 garlic clove

a small bunch of flatleaf parsley

1 oz. semi-dried tomatoes in olive oil, drained

1 small dried red chile, crumbled, seeds discarded (optional)

¼ cup each freshly grated Parmesan cheese and Pecorino cheese or ½ cup Parmesan

3–4 tablespoons extra virgin olive oil

freshly squeezed lemon juice or 1–2 tablespoons of crème fraîche or heavy cream, to taste

sea salt and freshly ground black pepper

Serves 4

One of the simplest and most delicious things you can do with a winter squash is cut it into wedges and roast it. The roasting emphasizes the sweetness and chestnutty denseness of the squash and lends itself to a zesty, full-flavored pesto such as this one, made from pumpkin seeds rather than the more usual pine nuts. Kabocha, Crown Prince, and Red Kuri squashes are particularly good roasted, but so is good old Butternut.

Preheat the oven to 400°F. Cut the squash into good-size wedges, discarding the seeds and pith as you go. Put it on a baking sheet, season, drizzle with some olive oil (about 1 tablespoon per wedge) and scatter over a few torn sage leaves. Roast, uncovered, in the preheated oven until tender, about 35–40 minutes, basting once with the oil.

Meanwhile, make the pesto. Toast the pumpkin seeds in a dry skillet over low heat for a few minutes. Do not allow them to burn. In a food processor or grinder, process the pumpkin seeds, garlic, parsley, tomatoes, and chile to make a rough paste. Add the cheese and then the oil, enough to make a spoonable pesto. Taste the pesto and add a squeeze of lemon juice to sharpen or crème fraîche to soften the flavor according to taste.

Serve immediately with the roasted squash wedges.

grilled zucchini, halloumi, & fava beans with tomato & mint dressing

3 medium zucchini (about 10–12 oz.), cut into 1½-inch slices

6 tablespoons extra virgin olive oil

4–5 oz. fresh shelled or frozen fava beans

½–1 tablespoon red wine vinegar

1–2 pinches ground roasted cumin seeds

2 teaspoons very finely chopped shallot or red onion

2 large tomatoes, skinned, seeded, and finely diced

1 tablespoon chopped mint leaves, plus extra to garnish

a pinch of sugar (optional)

6–8 oz. halloumi cheese, cut into slices about 2 inches thick

sea salt and freshly ground black pepper

a ridged, stovetop grill pan (optional)

Serves 2

Served with some crusty bread to mop up the dressing, this makes a tasty light lunch or supper, especially in summer when all the ingredients are at their best. That said, I must confess that more often than not I make this with frozen baby fava or lima beans, which are good all year round.

Toss the zucchini slices with 1 tablespoon of the oil. Bring a large saucepan of water to a boil, throw in the beans and cook for 5 minutes (3 minutes for frozen beans). Drain, refresh under cold water, then skin the beans if they are large.

Whisk the remaining oil and ½ tablespoon vinegar in a salad bowl. Add the cumin, salt and pepper, and more vinegar to taste. Whisk in the shallot, tomatoes, and mint, then add the sugar if you think it is necessary. Add the still-warm beans.

Cook the zucchini slices in a ridged stovetop grill pan or under a preheated hot broiler until tender and marked with brown, but not falling apart, about 2–3 minutes on each side. Toss, while still warm, in the dressing along with the beans.

Grill or broil the halloumi slices for about 2–3 minutes on each side until browned. Arrange on plates, then toss and add the dressed salad. Garnish with a few torn mint leaves and serve immediately.

tuna carpaccio and zucchini ribbons with soy & sesame dressing

a 14-oz piece of tuna in a neat "log", trimmed of all skin

2 tablespoons very finely chopped cilantro

sea salt and freshly ground black pepper

vegetable oil, for sautéing

for the dressing and salad

¼ cup olive oil or peanut oil

1 garlic clove, peeled and bruised

grated zest and freshly squeezed juice of 1 unwaxed lime

½–1 teaspoon finely chopped and seeded red chile (optional)

a thumb-size piece of fresh ginger, peeled and shredded

½ teaspoon honey

soy sauce and toasted sesame oil, to taste

4 small zucchini, topped and tailed

a small handful of sprouted seeds or shoots, such as cress, coriander, alfalfa, or pea shoots

a handful of peppery salad greens, such as arugula, baby mustard, and mizuna

toasted sesame seeds, to serve

Serves 4

The sweet, nutty crunch of raw zucchini works well with the smooth texture of wafer-thin slices of tuna, making this a great summer dish, as young zucchini are at their sweetest then. It goes without saying that you should seek out the best, freshest tuna you can find.

Rub the tuna with a few drops of oil and season well. Heat a ridged, stovetop grill pan or non-stick skillet over high heat until very hot, then sear the tuna quickly on all sides, It should brown on the outside, but appear cooked for only ⅛ inch around the edge. Remove from the heat, let cool a little, then roll the tuna in the chopped cilantro to cover. Let cool completely, wrap in plastic wrap, and chill well in the fridge.

Meanwhile, put the oil for the dressing in a bowl and add the garlic, a pinch or two of grated lime zest, and the chile (if using). Leave on one side while the tuna chills. Heat about ⅛ inch of oil in a small skillet over medium heat. When hot, add the ginger and cook briefly (just 30–60 seconds) until golden and crisp. Drain on paper towels.

When ready to serve, remove and discard the garlic from the dressing, then whisk in the honey and 2 teaspoons lime juice. Add a few drops of soy and sesame oil to taste and season with salt, pepper, and more lime juice.

Unwrap the tuna—cut wafer-thin slices across the grain and lay these, overlapping, on four plates. Using a vegetable peeler, cut long, thin ribbons of zucchini, directly into a salad bowl. Add the sprouts and the salad greens and toss with most of the dressing. Add a pile of salad to each plate, sprinkle over the fried ginger and sesame seeds, drizzle with the remaining dressing and serve immediately.

soups and salads

roasted squash, chick pea, & chorizo soup

1 lb. squash, peeled, seeded, and cut into ½-inch dice

5 tablespoons olive oil

1–2 pinches dried hot pepper flakes, crushed

1 large onion, finely diced

2 carrots, diced

2 celery ribs, sliced

6 oz. chorizo or other spicy cooking sausage, peeled and diced

1 red chile, seeded and finely chopped

2 garlic cloves, thinly sliced

a small of bunch of flatleaf parsley, stalks and leaves separated, both chopped

1 teaspoon each crushed cumin seeds and coriander seeds

2 tablespoons chopped oregano or 1½ teaspoons dried

1 x 7-oz can chopped tomatoes

1 x 14-oz can chick peas, drained and rinsed

5 cups vegetable stock

freshly squeezed lemon juice, to taste (optional)

sea salt and freshly ground black pepper

Serves 4–5

Roasting the squash adds depth of flavor and sweetness to this rustic soup, which warms the soul with its brick red and orange colors and robust, spicy flavors. Serve it with good crusty bread and all you need is a salad afterwards for a complete meal. This soup is inspired by a recipe from Sam and Sam Clark's *Moro: The Cookbook.*

Preheat the oven to 375°F. Put the squash on a baking sheet and toss with 2 tablespoons of oil. Season with salt and pepper and sprinkle over the hot pepper flakes. Roast in the preheated oven, stirring once or twice, until tender and browned, about 35–40 minutes.

Meanwhile, heat the remaining oil in a large saucepan and add the onion with a pinch of salt. Turn the heat to low, cover, and cook gently, stirring occasionally, for 10–15 minutes until tender. Add the carrots, celery and chorizo and cook, uncovered, for a further 5–7 minutes until beginning to brown. Add the fresh chile, garlic, chopped parsley stalks, and crushed spices. Stir-fry for another 4–5 minutes. Add the oregano, tomatoes, chick peas, and stock and bring to a boil. Reduce the heat and simmer gently for 10–12 minutes until the vegetables are tender. Stir in the roasted squash.

Process or liquidize about half the soup to give a coarse purée, then return it to the saucepan and reheat. Check the seasoning, adding more salt and/or lemon juice to taste. Finally, stir in the chopped parsley leaves and serve piping hot.

spicy pumpkin & coconut soup with ginger & lime

2 tablespoons sunflower oil

1½ lbs. pumpkin or squash, peeled, seeded and cut into chunks

a bunch of scallions, chopped

a 2-inch piece of fresh ginger, peeled and chopped

2 garlic cloves, chopped

2–3 red chiles, seeded and chopped, plus extra slices to garnish

2 lemongrass stalks, spilt lengthways

a large bunch of cilantro, stalks and leaves separated

5 cups vegetable or chicken stock

1 x 14-oz. can coconut milk

2–3 tablespoons Thai fish sauce

freshly squeezed juice of 1–2 limes

crème fraîche or sour cream, to serve

Serves 6

This beautiful orange and green soup with its sweet-sour flavor and hint of chile heat makes an exotic start to a special meal. Despite the richness of the coconut milk, the sharpness of the lime keeps it tasting light. You can use any orange-fleshed winter squash or cooking pumpkin for this recipe.

Heat the oil in a large saucepan and, over low heat, sweat the pumpkin and onions with a pinch of salt until soft but not browned, about 15–20 minutes.

Meanwhile, put the ginger, garlic, chiles, lemongrass, and cilantro stalks in another saucepan with the stock and simmer gently, covered, for 20–25 minutes. Let the stock cool slightly, then liquidize and sieve into the saucepan with the pumpkin mixture, pressing hard on the contents of the sieve to extract maximum flavor. Discard the debris in the sieve, then purée the liquid again with the pumpkin mixture until smooth.

Return the soup to the rinsed-out saucepan, add the coconut milk, 2 tablespoons fish sauce, and the juice of 1 lime, then reheat, stirring all the time, to just below boiling point. Adjust the seasoning, adding more fish sauce and lime juice to taste. Chop most of the cilantro leaves finely and stir into the soup (keep a few leaves to scatter over the soup at the end). Heat for a few minutes, but do not allow to boil.

Serve piping hot, topped with a spoonful of crème fraîche and scattered with the reserved coriander leaves and/or some extra red chile slices.

roasted squash & tomato soup with cumin & rosemary

5 tablespoons extra virgin olive oil, plus extra to drizzle

1 large sweet yellow onion, thickly sliced

1 teaspoon crushed cumin seeds, plus extra ground cumin to taste

1 lb. ripe tomatoes, skinned and halved

1 lb. prepared squash, cut into 1-inch chunks

2 medium red bell peppers, halved and deseeded

a small head of garlic, cloves separated but left unpeeled

2–3 teaspoons balsamic vinegar

leaves from 2 small rosemary sprigs, removed from the stalk and very finely chopped

½ teaspoon paprika

5 cups vegetable stock

freshly squeezed lime juice, to taste (optional)

a pinch of crushed, roasted cumin seeds, to serve

sea salt and freshly ground black pepper

Serves 4

A gorgeously colored and deep-flavored soup to make in the autumn when pumpkins, squashes, bell peppers, and tomatoes are at their very best and most seasonal. The cumin, rosemary, and paprika add a smoky flavor that seems to fit the mood of the season. This is delicious served with some chile cornbread or a loaf studded with intense nuggets of sun-dried tomato.

Preheat the oven to 400°F. Grease a baking sheet with 1 tablespoon of the oil. Put the onion slices at one end and scatter over the crushed cumin. Arrange the tomatoes, cut-side-uppermost, over the onions. Put the squash and bell peppers at the other end of the baking sheet with the garlic. Drizzle the vinegar over the tomatoes, season everything with a little salt and some black pepper and finally drizzle the remaining oil over everything. Roast, uncovered, in the preheated oven for 50–60 minutes, stirring the squash once. Remove from the oven and set aside to cool.

Pop the garlic cloves out of their skins into a large saucepan. Scrape all the roasted vegetables into the pan with the oil and add the rosemary and paprika. Stir over low heat for 2–3 minutes and then add the stock and bring to a boil. Reduce the heat and let simmer gently for 5–6 minutes. Let cool a little then process or liquidize until smooth. Adjust the seasoning with more cumin, salt and/or lime juice as necessary.

Serve piping hot, drizzled with a little extra oil and with a sprinkling of crushed roasted cumin.

grilled zucchini salad with sweet-sour dressing

1 lb. zucchini, topped, tailed and cut into long, thin strips or roundels

¼ cup extra virgin olive oil

1–2 pinches ground cumin or ground allspice

1–2 garlic cloves, finely chopped

1 teaspoon honey

1 tablespoon balsamic vinegar, plus extra to taste

a small bunch of mint, leaves only, chopped

4 tablespoons pine nuts, lightly toasted

sea salt and freshly ground black pepper

a ridged, stovetop grill pan

Serves 4

This is best served at room temperature rather than chilled and is excellent with grilled lamb, pork, chicken, or a "meaty" fish such as swordfish. It looks very pretty if you can use a mixture of green zucchini and yellow summer squash or tender little Pattypan. For a leafier salad, toss in a handful of wild arugula, mizuna, or baby spinach just before serving.

Toss the zucchini with 1 tablespoon of the oil and the cumin and season with salt and black pepper. Heat a ridged, stovetop grill pan until hot and cook the zucchini until just tender and striped with brown, about 4 minutes each side for 2-inch thick slices. As each batch is cooked, put it in a bowl.

In a small saucepan, heat the remaining oil very gently with the garlic—it should barely bubble and the garlic must not brown. After about 3–4 minutes, stir in the honey and vinegar, turn up the heat and let it bubble, then add 1 tablespoon cold water and beat with a fork to emulsify. Swirl in the mint and pine nuts, pour it over the zucchini and toss to mix. Season to taste with salt and pepper and a few extra drops of vinegar.

Let stand for about 10 minutes, toss again and serve.

roasted squash, chicken, & lentil salad with preserved lemon dressing

2 cups green lentils, preferably French "Le Puy" lentils

2 bay leaves

2–3 shallots, peeled

1 Butternut squash, peeled, seeded and cut into 1–2-inch chunks or slices

6 oz. cherry tomatoes

8–9 tablespoons extra virgin olive oil

1 large fennel bulb, trimmed and cut into ½-inch pieces, feathery tops reserved and chopped

1–2 teaspoons whole grain Dijon mustard

½ teaspoon honey

tarragon white wine vinegar or freshly squeezed lemon juice, to taste

4 tablespoons finely chopped flatleaf parsley

2–3 tablespoons chopped, preserved lemon (rind only)

1 small freshly roasted chicken (about 3½–4½ lbs.), carved and torn into shreds, skin discarded

a handful or arugula or baby spinach leaves, to serve

sea salt and freshly ground black pepper

Serves 6–8

I cannot tell you how good this combination of sweet squash, sharp lemon and earthy lentils is. It's best made with a freshly roasted chicken, but it can be made in advance for a picnic or party. You'll need to roast a whole chicken for this, stuffing it with a halved lemon and some garlic cloves and basting with a little olive oil and lemon.

Preheat the oven to 375°F. Rinse the lentils and put them in a saucepan with the bay leaves and one shallot, halved. Cover with cold water, bring to a boil and then simmer gently until cooked, about 30–40 minutes.

Meanwhile, toss the squash and tomatoes with 2 tablespoons of the oil on a baking sheet, season with salt and black pepper and roast, uncovered, in the preheated oven, stirring once, until tender and browned. The tomatoes should be collapsed but still juicy.

Heat 1½–2 tablespoons of the remaining oil in a skillet. Add the fennel with a pinch of salt and sauté it gently until softened but still with a bite, about 5–6 minutes.

Chop the remaining shallot(s) finely. In a bowl, whisk the remaining oil, mustard and honey together and add tarragon vinegar or lemon juice to taste (about 2–3 teaspoons). Season well with salt and black pepper. When the lentils are cooked, drain well and toss, while still warm, with the dressing. Toss in the roasted squash, tomatoes, fennel, parsley, the reserved fennel tops, the preserved lemon, and chicken pieces. Adjust the seasoning to taste and toss in the arugula just before turning onto a serving platter.

raw zucchini salad with lemon dressing, feta cheese, & toasted walnuts

3½ oz. fresh walnut halves

3 tablespoons extra virgin olive oil (or use 2 of olive oil and one of lemon-scented olive oil)

finely grated zest of ½ small unwaxed lemon

honey and freshly squeezed lemon juice, to taste

1 tablespoon light cream or crème fraîche

2 teaspoons chopped oregano or marjoram

1 tablespoon snipped chives

6 baby zucchini, topped and tailed

a large handful of baby spinach leaves

6½ oz. feta cheese, crumbled

sea salt and freshly ground black pepper

chive flowers, to garnish (optional)

Serves 4

Young zucchini, especially when freshly harvested, have a sweet, nutty taste and a lovely crunch when used raw. A mixture of varieties—green, pale green, and yellow—looks fresh and summery. Serve as an appetizer or to accompany broiled chicken or a vegetarian tart. A few chive flowers look lovely sprinkled on top in summer.

Preheat the oven to 350°F. Toast the walnuts on a baking sheet for 5–6 minutes, watching them closely so that they do not burn. Rub them in a dry, clean kitchen towel to remove any loose skin, crumble roughly and set aside.

Put the oil in a large salad bowl and add the lemon zest. Whisk in ½ teaspoon honey and 2 teaspoons lemon juice, then season with salt and pepper. Taste and add more honey and/or lemon juice as needed, then whisk in the cream, oregano, and chives.

Slice the zucchini very thinly directly into the dressing, add the baby spinach and toss to mix. (Do not toss the zucchini with the dressing too far in advance or they lose their crunchiness.) Divide between plates and top with the crumbled feta and walnuts. Sprinkle with chive flowers (if using) and serve immediately.

rice, pasta, and grains

pasta with zucchini, mint, lemon, & cream

3 tablespoons unsalted butter

10–12 oz. small zucchini, ends trimmed and cut into chunky matchsticks

7 oz. pasta of your choice

½ cup dry vermouth, such as Noilly Prat (optional)

⅔ cup heavy cream or crème fraîche

finely grated zest of 1 large unwaxed lemon

freshly squeezed lemon juice, to taste

2 tablespoons chopped mint

3–4 tablespoons toasted pine nuts

a few squash blossoms, to serve (optional)

sea salt and freshly ground black pepper

Serves 2

This makes a deliciously summery pasta that's full of flavor. You can make it with either green or yellow zucchini (the smaller the better), or you could use little Pattypan summer squashes. You could also toss some shredded golden yellow squash blossoms in at the very last moment to barely wilt in the heat of the pasta.

Melt the butter in a skillet over low heat and add the zucchini and a pinch of salt. Cook gently for about 10 minutes until tender but barely browned.

Meanwhile, bring a large saucepan of salted water to a boil and cook the pasta according to the package instructions. Drain, reserving a little of the pasta cooking water. Turn up the heat under the zucchini and add the vermouth (if using) or 4–5 tablespoons of the cooking water and let it bubble and evaporate. Add the cream and lemon zest, and again let it bubble, reduce, and thicken slightly. If it reduces too much, add another 1–2 tablespoons cooking water. Sharpen with a squeeze or two of lemon juice as necessary and toss with the pasta and mint.

Serve immediately on warmed plates with a grinding of black pepper and a sprinkling of toasted pine nuts.

pasta with pan-fried squash, walnut, & parsley sauce

1¼ cups fresh walnut halves

2–3 fat garlic cloves, peeled

5 tablespoons olive oil

1 tablespoon walnut oil

5 tablespoons heavy cream or crème fraîche

a small bunch of flatleaf parsley

freshly squeezed lemon juice, to taste

1½ lbs. prepared squash, cut into ½-inch thick slices or chunks

1–2 pinches dried hot pepper flakes, crushed

14 oz. pasta of your choice

freshly grated nutmeg, to taste

sea salt and freshly ground black pepper

freshly grated Parmesan, to serve

Serves 4

This is a lovely and unusual pasta dish, well-suited to the season of mists and mellow fruitfulness, when walnuts and all kinds of orange-fleshed squashes will be at their best. Traditionally, a version of this walnut sauce is served with pappardelle pasta in northern Italy, but it is good with other shapes too, including, strange though it may seem (and distinctly unItalian), whole wheat spaghetti.

Preheat the oven to 350°F. Put the walnuts on a baking sheet and toast them in the preheated oven for 5–6 minutes, making sure they don't burn. Turn them onto a dry, clean kitchen towel and rub vigorously to remove as much of the skin as possible. Chop one-third of the nuts roughly and set aside then put the remaining nuts in a food processor. Blanch the garlic in boiling water for 2–3 minutes, drain and rinse. Put the garlic in the processor with the walnuts, add 2 tablespoons olive oil, the walnut oil, and cream. Whizz to make a paste. Set aside a third of the parsley, then whizz the remaining two-thirds into the sauce. Chop the reserved parsley and set aside. Leave the sauce in the processor until needed.

In a large frying pan, heat the remaining olive oil over medium heat, add the squash and hot pepper flakes and cook, turning the squash now and then, until it is tender and lightly browned, about 10–12 minutes. Meanwhile, bring a large saucepan of salted water to a boil and cook the pasta according to the package instructions.

When the pasta is cooked, drain, reserving 4–5 tablespoons of the cooking water. Whizz enough of this water into the sauce to make it creamy, then season with salt, pepper, and a little nutmeg. Toss the pasta with the squash, remaining walnuts and parsley and a little of the sauce. Serve the Parmesan and remaining sauce at the table.

pumpkin risotto with pancetta & sage

3 tablespoons unsalted butter

2 tablespoons olive oil, plus extra for frying the sage leaves

1 medium, sweet yellow onion, finely chopped

1 celery rib, finely chopped

5 oz. pancetta, cut into lardons

1 lb. prepared squash or pumpkin, cut into ½–1-inch dice

4–5 sage leaves, torn, plus a small handful extra to garnish

1¾ cups Arborio or Carnaroli risotto rice

⅔ cup dry white wine

5 cups vegetable or chicken stock

½ cup freshly grated Parmesan cheese, plus extra to serve

sea salt and freshly ground black pepper

Serves 4

Despite the name, you can use any well-flavored winter squash for this recipe—Butternut is fine. If using pumpkin, go for an Italian or French variety such as Tonda, Zucca di Napoli or a Musque de Provence. The common orange Halloween or Cinderella pumpkin is too stringy and watery for this sublime autumnal risotto.

Heat half the butter and 1 tablespoon of the oil in a deep skillet. Add the onion, celery and a pinch of salt. Cover the pan, turn the heat down low and let the onion and celery cook slowly, stirring once or twice until softened and golden but not browned. Add the pancetta and cook for another 5 minutes before adding the squash. Cook gently, uncovered, until the squash is half cooked, about 6 minutes, adding the torn sage leaves for the last 1–2 minutes.

Add the rice and 1 teaspoon salt to the onion and squash mixture. Cook gently, turning the rice with the buttery vegetables, until it begins to look translucent. Turn up the heat, add the wine and cook at a medium simmer, stirring frequently with a wooden spoon, until the wine has evaporated.

Meanwhile, heat the stock in a large saucepan and keep it hot. When the wine has evaporated, add 2 ladlefuls of the hot stock to the rice mixture and stir until it has all been absorbed by the rice. Continue to add more stock, 1–2 ladlefuls at a time, whilst stirring continuously, as this releases the creamy starch in the rice. Repeat until all the stock has been absorbed and the rice is tender but still al dente, about 16–18 minutes. When cooked, stir in the remaining butter and the grated Parmesan. Stir, cover and leave to rest for a few minutes. Heat a little oil in a small skillet over medium heat. When hot, add the remaining sage leaves and cook for a few seconds only until just crisp. Drain on paper towels. Serve the risotto on warmed plates, with a scattering of sage leaves, and offer more grated Parmesan at the table.

torta di riso con zucchini (rice cake with zucchini)

a good pinch of saffron threads

5 cups vegetable or chicken stock

3 tablespoons dry white breadcrumbs

1 cup freshly grated Parmesan cheese

2 tablespoons butter

1 tablespoon olive oil

1 medium onion, finely chopped

1–2 garlic cloves, finely chopped

14 oz. zucchini

1 tablespoon chopped tarragon, plus 2–3 sprigs

2 cups Arborio or Carnaroli risotto rice

5–6 oz. fresh shelled or frozen fava beans

2 eggs

⅓ cup light cream

a small bunch of chervil or curly parsley, chopped

a handful of squash blossoms, shredded (optional)

sea salt and freshly ground black pepper

a 22–23-cm springform cake tin, buttered and lined with baking paper

Serves 6

Italian cookery books often suggest ways to use up left-over risotto and this is one such recipe. But it is worth cooking the rice from scratch for this dish as, unlike risotto, the whole thing can be prepared well in advance, then baked at the last moment. As with most Italian rice dishes, it is best served warm rather than piping hot.

Preheat the oven to 375°F. Put the saffron in a small bowl. Heat the stock in a saucepan and add 2–3 tablespoons to the saffron. Mix the breadcrumbs with 2 tablespoons of Parmesan and use this mixture to thickly dust a buttered cake pan. Reserve any excess.

Heat the butter and oil in a large skillet with a lid. Gently sauté the onion with a pinch of salt, covered, until soft and golden but not browned, about 10–12 minutes. Add the garlic, zucchini, and tarragon sprigs and cook, stirring once or twice, until the zucchini begin to soften. Add the rice and stir until it looks translucent, then add 1 teaspoon salt, the saffron and stock. Bring to a boil, stir well, then cover tightly, reduce the heat to low and cook, without stirring, for about 15 minutes until the stock is completely absorbed.

Meanwhile, blanch the beans in boiling, salted water for 4–5 minutes (3 minutes for frozen beans), drain, then, if the beans are any larger than your thumbnail, peel off the outer skin. When the rice is cooked, take it off the heat, cover with a dry, clean kitchen towel, then cover with the lid and leave to steam for 5–10 minutes. Beat the eggs and cream in a bowl and then beat in all the chopped herbs. Add the rice, remaining Parmesan, the cooked beans, and the shredded squash blossoms (if using). Check the seasoning, spoon the mixture into the prepared pan, level the top and then sprinkle any remaining breadcrumb and Parmesan mixture over the top. Bake in the preheated oven for 50–60 minutes. Let cool in the tin for 10–15 minutes before turning out and serving, cut into generous wedges.

pumpkin gnocchi with buttery sage breadcrumbs

a starchy, dry-fleshed pumpkin or squash, such as Kabocha or Crown Prince (about 2 lbs.), halved and seeded

1 lb. medium floury potatoes, unpeeled, washed, and pricked

1½ cups all-purpose flour, sifted with ½ teaspoon baking powder, plus extra flour as needed

⅓ cup fine semolina, plus extra for dusting

½ cup freshly grated Parmesan cheese, plus extra to serve

freshly grated nutmeg, to taste

1 stick unsalted butter

1 garlic clove, peeled and halved

¼ cup white breadcrumbs from day-old bread

10 sage leaves, shredded

sea salt and freshly ground black pepper

Serves 4

These gnocchi are light and yet deeply satisfying. Do not prepare them too far ahead of cooking or they will become wet and sticky. To prepare in advance, open freeze them on a well-floured sheet then pack in freezer bags. They can be stored for up to six months and will cook well from frozen.

Preheat the oven to 400°F. Line a baking sheet with lightly oiled foil. Put the pumpkin, cut-side down, and the potatoes on the tray. Bake in the preheated oven for 1 hour, until soft. (Check the squash after 40 minutes—if cooked, remove it and continue baking the potatoes.) When cool enough to handle, scrape the squash flesh off the skin and do the same with the potato. Using a ricer or sieve, purée the vegetables into a bowl. Do not use a food processor as it will make the potatoes too gluey. While the puréed vegetables are still warm, work in the flour and semolina using a fork. Add more flour as necessary to make a malleable mixture. Work in half the Parmesan and season well with salt, pepper, and nutmeg.

Dust a work surface with semolina. Take about one-third of the mixture and roll it out to form a long, thin sausage shape about ¾-inch thick. Cut into 1-inch lengths. Roll each piece along the tines of a fork, then in a little semolina and set on a kitchen towel-covered tray, dusted with more semolina. Repeat with the remaining mixture.

Bring a large saucepan of salted water to a boil. Heat half the butter in a skillet over medium heat with the garlic. Let the garlic sizzle for a few minutes, then add the breadcrumbs and half the sage. Fry gently until the breadcrumbs turn crisp and golden brown. Discard the garlic. In a separate pan, melt the remaining butter, add the remaining sage and keep warm. When the water boils, turn it down to a simmer and cook the gnocchi in batches until they bob to the surface, then cook for 1–2 minutes more. Use a slotted spoon to transfer them to a warmed serving dish. Toss with the butter and sage, then with the breadcrumbs. Serve immediately, offering extra Parmesan.

roasted squash with leek & barley pilaf

Squash and leeks share a similar vegetable sweetness that makes them very good bedfellows. The comforting feather mattress here is the earthy nuttiness of barley, but you could also cook spelt grains (farro) in the same way. All it needs is a green salad in a mustardy sour cream dressing, with a few toasted walnuts tossed through.

1¼ cups pearl barley

1 bay leaf

1 Butternut or a large wedge of a similar winter squash

¼ cup olive oil

1 tablespoon small thyme sprigs

1–2 pinches dried hot pepper flakes, to taste

2 tablespoons butter

2–3 celery ribs, sliced

4 leeks, thickly sliced

8 oz. brown mushrooms, sliced

2 carrots, coarsely shredded

½–¾ cup vegetable stock

a handful of flatleaf parsley, roughly chopped

3 tablespoons lightly toasted pumpkin seeds (optional)

6–8 oz. Taleggio or Fontina cheese, thinly sliced

Serves 4

Rinse the barley well, then put it in a large saucepan with the bay leaf. Cover generously with water and bring to a boil. Reduce the heat and simmer gently, part-covered, for about 30–40 minutes until tender. Drain and set aside until needed.

Preheat the oven to 400°F. Cut the squash into 4–8 wedges. Do not peel it but scoop out the seeds. Rub with half the oil and put on a baking sheet, season with salt and pepper, and scatter over half the thyme and the hot pepper flakes. Roast, uncovered, in the preheated oven for about 40 minutes until tender and browned.

Meanwhile, heat the remaining oil and half the butter in a large skillet and cook the celery gently for 5 minutes. Add the leeks and most of the remaining thyme and cook for another 4–5 minutes, stirring once or twice. Add the mushrooms and cook over medium heat until they begin to brown, then toss in the carrots and cook for 1–2 minutes only. Add the barley and stir through, then add sufficient stock to make the grains moist and reheat thoroughly. Check the seasoning, then stir in the parsley, pumpkin seeds (if using), and remaining butter.

To serve, top the squash with the sliced cheese and remaining few thyme sprigs, grind over some pepper, and either let it melt in the oven or under a hot broiler until it bubbles. Serve immediately with the barley pilaf.

entrées

pumpkin fondue

1 medium red or orange pumpkin, about 10–12 inches in diameter, or 4 small, round Gold Nugget squash or similar

3–4 tablespoons olive oil

a few torn thyme sprigs or sage leaves

sea salt and freshly ground black pepper

for the fondue

2 teaspoons potato flour or cornstarch

1¼ cups dry white wine, such as Riesling or Grüner Veltliner, or hard cider

1 garlic clove, peeled and halved

1 bay leaf

14 oz. Gruyere (or see other cheeses mentioned), derinded and thinly sliced or shredded

2 tablespoon Kirsch (optional)

8–10 oz. Taleggio or Fontina cheese, derinded and thinly sliced or grated

¼ cup heavy cream or crème fraîche

Serves 4

Serving fondue in a baked pumpkin shell is not just about fun presentation—the sweet, tender flesh is wonderful with the salty, sharp richness of the cheese. Either use a whole, large pumpkin for everyone to dip into or small individual squashes. Serve with cubes of crusty bread for dipping and spoons for scraping the baked squash from the shell. The cheese you use is up to you. I like a mixture of a Gruyere-like cheese (Emmental, Beaufort, or Irish Coolea) with a softer cheese such as Taleggio or Fontina.

Preheat the oven to 375°F. Cut a lid off the pumpkin or the squashes and, if necessary, take a thin slice off the base so that the shell(s) will stand upright without wobbling.

Scoop out the seeds and enough flesh to leave a shell about 1 inch thick (small squash are fine as they are, just remove the seeds). Rub with the oil inside and out, season with salt and pepper, add a few herb sprigs to the cavity, and bake in the preheated oven for about 50 minutes for a large pumpkin or 40 minutes for small squash. Bake the lids as well, if liked, for around 20–25 minutes, depending on size.

Meanwhile, make the cheese fondue. Mix the potato flour with 2–3 tablespoons of the wine and set aside. Put the remaining wine in a medium-sized, heavy-based saucepan over medium heat and bring to a boil. Simmer for 2–3 minutes, then add the garlic and bay leaf and reduce the heat. Add the Gruyere cheese and, stirring all the time, allow it to melt. When melted, remove and discard the garlic and bay leaf then stir in the potato flour mixture and the Kirsch (if using) until smooth. Add the Taleggio and stir frequently over low heat until the cheese melts. Add the cream, season to taste, and stir over the heat until you have a smooth, velvety texture.

To serve, pour the fondue into the baked shell(s), cover with the lid(s), if using, and carry to the table.

fish, pumpkin, & coconut curry

1 medium pumpkin or squash (about 2 lbs.), peeled, seeded, and cut into 1-inch slices

4 tablespoons safflower or peanut oil

2-inch piece of fresh ginger, peeled and chopped

4 garlic cloves, chopped

a small bunch of cilantro, stalks and leaves separated

3–4 red chiles, seeded

1 large onion, halved and sliced

10 oz. tomatoes, skinned, seeded, and chopped

1⅔ cup fish stock

2 green bell peppers, seeded and sliced

1 x 14-oz can coconut milk

2–4 teaspoons tamarind paste

2 lbs. thick, white fish fillets, cut into chunks

1½ lbs. shelled, uncooked shrimp, deveined

sea salt and freshly ground black pepper

spice mix

4 cloves

1 teaspoon coriander seeds

2 teaspoons cumin seeds

½ teaspoon black peppercorns

1 teaspoon ground turmeric

Serves 4–6 depending on your accompaniments

The sweet, rich flavor of roasted pumpkin works so well with Indian spices in this light, fragrant curry. The fish you use needs to be one that will cut into chunks and not break up on cooking—monkfish is good. Serve with a green vegetable, such as shredded cabbage, stir-fried with onion, ginger, and kalonji (nigella) seeds and some saffron rice. It's also good with Indian naan bread and salad greens.

Preheat the oven to 400°F. Toss the pumpkin with 2 tablespoons of the oil and some salt and pepper. Transfer to a baking sheet and roast in the preheated oven, stirring once or twice, until browned and tender, about 35–40 minutes.

Meanwhile, in a small dry, skillet over medium heat, toast the cloves, coriander seeds, and half the cumin seeds for 2–3 minutes until fragrant. Let cool, then grind in a mill or mortar and pestle with the black peppercorns to make a powder. Stir in the ground turmeric. Blend together the ginger, garlic, cilantro stalks, and 2–3 chiles with 3 tablespoons water to form a paste, then blend in 2 teaspoons of the dry spice mixture.

In a saucepan, very gently sauté the onion in the remaining oil with a pinch of salt for 10 minutes until softened but not browned. Add the remaining cumin seeds and sauté for another 3–4 minutes, then add the ginger paste, turn up the heat and cook for 4–5 minutes until the liquid evaporates. Add the tomatoes and cook again for 3–4 minutes until the mixture looks dry. Stir in the stock and bell peppers and cook for 10 minutes. Add the coconut milk and 2 teaspoons tamarind. Let it bubble gently for a few minutes, then stir in seasoning and more tamarind to taste. Stir in the pumpkin and fish and let it gently cook for 5 minutes then add the shrimp and cook until they turn pink. Add more of the spice mixture to taste, stir in most of the chopped cilantro leaves and transfer to a serving dish. Sprinkle with the remaining cilantro and red chile, thinly sliced. Serve immediately.

lamb cutlets with zucchini, beans, & mint salsa verde

a small handful of mint leaves

a small handful of flatleaf parsley

2 garlic cloves, peeled and halved

1 tablespoon capers, soaked in cold water, then drained

1 green chile, seeded

10 tablespoons extra virgin olive oil

1–1½ tablespoons white wine vinegar, to taste

1–1½ teaspoons whole grain Dijon mustard, to taste

a 6-cutlet, French-trimmed rack of lamb

5 oz. cherry tomatoes

4 medium zucchini, trimmed and thickly sliced or cut into batons

a few thyme sprigs

1 x 14-oz can cannellini or flageolet beans (small French kidney beans), drained and rinsed

sea salt and freshly ground black pepper

a ridged, stovetop grill pan (optional)

Serves 2

Zucchini and lamb are a good match—they share a natural sweetness and they both work well with the sprightly flavor of mint. Any leftover salsa is delicious with other cooked vegetables such as steamed potatoes, cauliflower, or grilled eggplant.

Put the mint, parsley, garlic, capers, and chile in a food processor and whizz until well chopped. Gradually feed in sufficient oil through the funnel to make a thick but spoonable salsa. Scrape into a bowl and add vinegar and mustard to taste. Rub 2 tablespoons of the salsa over the lamb. Slip the lamb into a plastic bag and let marinate in the fridge for up to 6 hours. Cover the remaining salsa and refrigerate.

Preheat the oven to 425°F and take the lamb out of the fridge. Toss the tomatoes, zucchini, and thyme in 2 tablespoons of oil and season well. Transfer to a baking sheet and roast, uncovered, in the preheated oven for 20–25 minutes, stirring once. Scrape the marinade off the lamb. Heat a ridged, stovetop grill pan or heavy skillet until very hot. Cook the lamb, fat-side down, for 4–5 minutes until the fat is browned then transfer to a baking sheet and cook in the still-hot oven for 10–15 minutes, depending on how pink you like your lamb. Keep the lamb warm, tented in foil, and let it rest for 5–10 minutes before carving.

Meanwhile, heat the beans with the remaining oil in a saucepan. When hot, stir in 2 tablespoons of salsa, the tomatoes, and zucchini. Carve the rack into cutlets and serve on warmed plates with the beans and zucchini. Serve any remaining salsa on the side.

pork & zucchini meatballs with honeyed eggplant & yogurt dressing

1 lb. zucchini, trimmed

1 lb. ground pork

2 heaped tablespoons dry white breadcrumbs

1 teaspoon fennel seeds, crushed

1 red chile, seeded and finely chopped

1 fat garlic clove, finely chopped

zest of 1 small unwaxed lemon

1–2 teaspoons chopped lemon thyme or oregano

olive oil, for roasting and sautéing

1 large eggplant, cut into ½–1 inch cubes

1½ teaspoons cumin seeds

2 tablespoons honey

1–2 tablespoons chopped dill

½ teaspoon ground sumac (optional)

¾ cup Greek yogurt

2 unwaxed lemons, halved

seeds from 1 pomegranate

sea salt and freshly ground black pepper

Serves 4

The grated zucchini keeps these little meatballs light and moist. I've partnered them here with a warm salad of roasted eggplant and zucchini accompanied by a yogurt dressing, but you could also serve them more traditionally in a tomato sauce with pasta.

Coarsely grate about 6–7 oz. of the zucchini, toss with 1 teaspoon salt, then leave to drain in a colander for 45–60 minutes. Rinse, transfer to a dry, clean kitchen towel and squeeze dry. Put the pork, grated zucchini, breadcrumbs, crushed fennel seeds, chile, garlic, lemon zest, and thyme in a bowl with ½ teaspoon salt and a grinding of black pepper and mix thoroughly using your hands. Form into small balls the size of walnuts. Chill in the fridge until ready to cook.

Meanwhile, preheat the oven to 400°F. Cut the remaining zucchini into cubes of a similar size to the eggplant. Toss the zucchini and eggplant with 2 tablespoons olive oil and season well. Toast the cumin seeds in a small, dry skillet over low heat until fragrant, then crush in a mortar with a pestle. Sprinkle half over the vegetables and roast them, uncovered, in the preheated oven for about 30–35 minutes, stirring once, until tender and nicely browned. Drizzle over the honey, then roast for a further 5–7 minutes.

Turn into a bowl and toss with most of the dill and sumac (if using). Beat the yogurt with the remaining cumin, then season to taste. Cook the meatballs in very shallow oil in a non-stick skillet for about 8–10 minutes until browned on all sides and cooked through. Remove from the pan and keep warm. Wipe out the pan, then add the lemons, cut-side down, and cook briefly until browned and caramelized on the cut side. Top the salad with the remaining dill and the pomegranate seeds. Serve the meatballs piping hot, with the caramelized lemon halves and the salad and yogurt on the side.

spaghetti squash gratin with pancetta, mushrooms, & crème fraîche

1 spaghetti squash (about 1 lb.)

1 tablespoon each butter and olive oil, plus extra olive oil to drizzle

4–5 oz. pancetta, cubed

8 oz. brown mushrooms, sliced

2–3 tablespoons dry white wine or freshly squeezed lemon juice, to taste

2 tablespoons chopped parsley

1 teaspoon chopped thyme, plus a few sprigs

⅔ cup crème fraîche or sour cream

½–¾ cup grated Parmesan cheese

2–3 tablespoons fresh white breadcrumbs

sea salt and freshly ground black pepper

a ovenproof gratin or lasagne dish, buttered

Serves 3–4

Spaghetti squash has to be one of the strangest vegetables. On the outside it looks like a standard squash, but when cooked the interior separates into spaghetti-like strands. As it's lighter than pasta, it lends itself to richer treatment, as here.

Leave the squash whole and put it in a large saucepan with enough boiling water to cover. Boil for about 35–40 minutes, turning once during cooking, until tender when pierced with a skewer, then drain. Alternatively, halve it and stand it, cut-side down, in a baking dish with a few tablespoons of water and bake in a preheated oven at 375°F for about 45 minutes until tender. Leave until cool enough to handle, then scoop out and discard the seeds and fork out the strands of "spaghetti" into a colander. Let them drain until needed.

Heat the butter and oil in a skillet. Add the pancetta and sauté until just beginning to brown. Add the mushrooms and sauté gently until the moisture they give out has evaporated and they begin to brown. Add the wine or a squeeze of lemon juice and cook briskly to drive off the moisture before adding the parsley and half the chopped thyme. Transfer to a large bowl, add the drained spaghetti squash, season well, and toss to combine.

Preheat the oven to 375°F if necessary. Pile the squash mixture into the gratin dish. Stir the crème fraîche until smooth. Season with black pepper and half the Parmesan and spoon over the squash. Mix the remaining chopped thyme, Parmesan and breadcrumbs together and sprinkle over the top. Add a few thyme sprigs and a drizzle of oil and bake in the preheated oven for 20 minutes until bubbling and crusty brown. Serve immediately.

beef stew with squash, corn, & chile

2¼ lbs. beef chuck

1 teaspoon ground allspice

1 rounded teaspoon smoked Spanish paprika (pimentón)

4–6 tablespoons olive oil

4 garlic cloves, finely chopped

a small bunch of oregano

2 medium onions, sliced

2–3 red chiles, seeded and cut into thin strips, plus extra, finely sliced, to garnish

1 teaspoon cumin seeds, lightly crushed

1 x 14-oz. can chopped tomatoes

3 cups beef stock

a small piece of cinnamon stick and a strip of orange zest

1½ lbs. orange-fleshed squash or pumpkin, such as Butternut, Kabocha, or Calabaza, peeled, seeded, and cut into chunks

2 red bell peppers, seeded and cut into chunks

brown sugar, to taste (optional)

2 cups fresh or frozen corn kernels

½ oz. dark, bitter chocolate (70% cocoa minimum)

sea salt and freshly ground black pepper

Serves 6

Squash, corn, and chile form the holy trinity of southern States cooking. And here they are added to a beef stew that's packed with spicy flavor and given added richness by the last-minute addition of dark chocolate. You could serve this in a hollowed-out pumpkin shell for real impact.

Cut the beef into 2-inch pieces, discarding any excess fat. Put the beef in a sealable bag with the ground allspice and half the paprika. Add 2 tablespoons of the oil, half the garlic, a little salt, and some black pepper. Chop 1 tablespoon oregano finely and add it to the bag. Seal the bag, massage the marinade into the beef, and let marinate in the fridge for several hours.

When ready to cook, preheat the oven to 325°F. Scrape the marinade off the beef and reserve it. Dry the meat on paper towels. Heat the remaining oil in a skillet and brown the meat on all sides. Do this in batches, putting the beef into a flameproof casserole as you cook it. Reduce the heat, add the onions to the pan with a pinch of salt and cook gently for 10–15 minutes until soft and sweet. Add the chiles, remaining garlic, and the crushed cumin and sauté for another 3–4 minutes. Add the marinade and remaining paprika followed by the tomatoes and cook over medium heat for a few minutes. Add the stock, cinnamon, and orange zest, bring to a boil and pour over the beef in the casserole. Cover with a sheet of parchment paper followed by the lid to make a tight seal and cook in the preheated oven for about 1½ hours.

Stir in the squash and bell peppers. Check and adjust the seasoning, adding salt, pepper, or a pinch of sugar as necessary. Cook for a further 30 minutes at 350°F, stir in the corn, and cook for another 25–30 minutes. Make sure the squash is fully cooked. Remove the casserole from the oven and set over medium heat. Chop some of the remaining oregano leaves to give 1–2 teaspoons. Stir the chocolate and chopped oregano into the stew. Let it bubble for a few minutes, then serve scattered with the extra chile and a few sprigs of oregano.

chicken & butternut squash tagine with saffron

3 tablespoons each of butter and olive oil

1 teaspoon each crushed cumin seeds and coriander seeds

a piece of cinnamon stick

2 large onions, halved and thinly sliced

2 garlic cloves, chopped

1 teaspoon chopped fresh ginger

1 green chile, seeded and chopped, plus a little extra to taste

4 whole chicken legs, cut in 2, or a chicken cut into 8 pieces

2–3 bay leaves

2 teaspoons honey

2 tablespoons chopped preserved lemon (discard any pips), plus a little extra to taste

a small bunch of cilantro, stalks and leaves separated

1⅔ cup chicken stock

½ teaspoon smoked Spanish paprika (pimentón)

a squash (about 1½–2 lb.), peeled, seeded, and cut into small wedges or slices

a good pinch of saffron threads

⅓ cup blanched almonds, sautéd in a little butter until light brown

sea salt and freshly ground black pepper

Serves 4

This fragrant, Moroccan-inspired stew is heady with the scent of saffron and sharp with lemon, all of which works so well with the sweet density of the roasted squash. Serve with some buttered couscous. Just cover couscous with water or vegetable stock and let it absorb the liquid, fork through some melted butter, then reheat—either steaming in a cheesecloth-lined sieve or in the microwave.

Heat the butter and 1 tablespoon of the oil in a flameproof casserole or heavy-based skillet. Add the spices and cook over low heat for 2–3 minutes, then add the onions, garlic, ginger, and chile and cook gently for 5–6 minutes more. Add the chicken pieces and turn them in the juices for 1–2 minutes—do not let them brown. Add the bay leaves, honey, preserved lemon, and chopped cilantro stalks. Add the stock, ¼ teaspoon salt, black pepper to taste, and paprika. Bring to a boil then stir well, cover and cook very gently for about 45–50 minutes until the chicken is very tender.

Meanwhile, preheat the oven to 375°F. Toss the prepared squash in the remaining oil, season, and roast on a baking sheet until browned and tender, about 35–40 minutes. Soak the saffron in 2 tablespoons hot water and chop the cilantro leaves.

When the chicken is done, remove it to a serving dish and keep warm. Turn the heat up under the casserole and reduce the liquid by about half, then add the saffron and most of the coriander. Cook for a few minutes, then taste. Adjust the seasoning, adding a little more chile or preserved lemon to taste. Stir in the roasted squash and heat through. Spoon the squash and sauce over the chicken, sprinkle with the remaining cilantro and almonds and serve immediately.

squash, goat cheese, & sun-dried tomato tarts with parmesan pastry

for the pastry

1½ cups all-purpose flour

6 tablespoons unsalted butter, chilled

a pinch each of salt and cayenne pepper

1 cup freshly grated Parmesan cheese

1 egg yolk

for the filling

3 tablespoons olive oil

1 large onion, halved and thinly sliced

12 oz. prepared squash, diced

2 teaspoons finely chopped thyme leaves

5 oz. goat cheese, crumbled into roughly ½–1-inch pieces

3½ oz. sun-dried tomatoes in oil, drained and roughly chopped

¾ cup heavy cream

2 eggs

2 tablespoons snipped chives

sea salt and freshly ground black pepper

6 individual, 3½-inch metal tart pans with removable bottoms

Serves 6

This recipe brings together all the most delicious things that work well with the sweet, dense flesh of winter squash. Sharp goat cheese, salty Parmesan, caramelly sun-dried tomatoes and onion, and the scent of thyme all contrive to make this my favorite savory tart (probably). Best served just warm, rather than piping hot.

To make the pastry, put the flour, butter, salt, and cayenne pepper in a food processor and whizz until the mixture resembles breadcrumbs. Add the Parmesan, egg yolk, and 1½ tablespoons ice water and whizz again until it forms a dough. Shape the pastry dough into a smooth ball on a work surface, wrap in foil, and chill in the fridge for at least 40 minutes.

Preheat the oven to 375°F. Roll out the chilled pastry thinly and line 6 individual tart pans. Protect the sides with strips of foil, then chill for a further 30 minutes. Transfer to a baking sheet and cook in the preheated oven for 12 minutes. Remove the foil and return them to the oven to cook for another 5–6 minutes until pale brown.

To make the filling, heat the oil in a skillet and add the onion and a pinch of salt. Cover, reduce the heat to low and cook, stirring once or twice, for 10–12 minutes until softened but not browned. Add the squash and cook over medium heat, uncovered and stirring occasionally, until the squash is tender and lightly browned. Add the thyme, stir a few minutes more, then take off the heat and let cool. Arrange the squash, cheese, and tomatoes in the part-baked tart crusts. Beat together the cream and eggs, add the chives and season with salt and pepper. Carefully pour the mixture into the tart crusts, return them to the hot oven and cook for about 25–30 minutes until the custard is set and puffed up. Let cool slightly before serving.

zucchini pizza with rosemary & goat cheese

for the dough

2½ cups bread flour (or half and half with Italian 00 tipo flour), plus a little extra as necessary

½ teaspoon salt

1 teaspoon fast-action dry yeast

½ teaspoon sugar

¾ cup warm water, plus 1–2 tablespoons extra as necessary

1 tablespoon extra virgin olive oil

for the topping

3–4 tablespoons extra virgin olive oil, plus extra to drizzle

14 oz. sweet yellow onions, halved and thinly sliced

14 oz. zucchini, trimmed and thinly sliced

2 garlic cloves, thinly sliced

1 teaspoon very finely chopped rosemary leaves, plus a few extra small sprigs

2 tablespoons dry white wine or dry vermouth such as Noilly Prat

12–14 oz. goat cheese, Fontina, or mozzarella, thickly sliced

¼ cup pine nuts

sea salt and freshly ground black pepper

Makes 2 pizzas, each 12-inch diameter

Zucchini make a delicious topping for a pizza when cooked with mild, sweet onions, and flavored with rosemary and garlic. You could use mozzarella or Fontina if you prefer, but I like the slight chalkiness of goat cheese.

Put the flour in a warmed bowl and stir in the salt and yeast. Dissolve the sugar in the water, then stir that into the flour with the oil. Gradually bring the mixture together to make a dough, adding extra water as necessary if too dry and a little extra flour if too sticky. Form into a smooth, slightly sticky ball of dough, cover, then let rest for 10 minutes. Knead on a lightly floured or oiled surface for 5–6 minutes until smooth and elastic. Put back into the lightly oiled bowl, cover with plastic wrap and let rise at room temperature for about 1 hour until at least doubled in size. Knock it back to deflate, then cover and let it rise again while you make the topping.

Heat 3 tablespoons oil in a sauté pan with a lid. When hot, add the onions and a good pinch of salt. Stir, cover, and immediately reduce the heat to low. Cook, stirring once or twice, for 10 minutes until the onions have softened but not browned. Add the zucchini, garlic, and chopped rosemary. Continue to cook gently, covered, until the zucchini are soft but not breaking up. Add the extra oil if you need it. Uncover, turn up the heat a little and add the wine. Cook until the liquid evaporates, taste, and adjust the seasoning. Set aside to cool.

When the dough has risen for a second time, divide it in half and roll each piece out to make a 12-inch circular pizza base. Put both on well-floured baking sheets and keep covered in a warm, not hot, place. Preheat the oven to 425°F. When ready to cook, spread the onion and zucchini topping over the pizza bases, top with the cheese, add a few rosemary sprigs, and a scattering of pine nuts. Drizzle with 1–2 tablespoons oil per pizza and grind over some black pepper. Bake in the preheated oven for about 20–25 minutes until the edges are golden brown. Serve with an arugula salad.

baby squash stuffed with pine nuts, currants, lemon, & herbs

4 small acorn squashes or good-sized zucchini

1 tablespoon salted capers

¼ cup currants

1 medium onion, finely chopped

5–6 tablespoons extra virgin olive oil

2–3 garlic cloves, finely chopped

1¼ cups fresh white breadcrumbs

2 tablespoons chopped flatleaf parsley

2 tablespoons chopped mint leaves

1–2 teaspoons grated lemon zest

½ cup freshly grated Parmesan cheese

⅓ cup pine nuts, lightly toasted

1 egg, beaten (optional)

1 tablespoon freshly squeezed lemon juice

sea salt and freshly ground black pepper

an ovenproof baking dish, oiled

Serves 4

The flavors here are Italian in style, specifically Sicilian, and I love the unexpected mix of sweet currants with the saltiness of the capers and cheese. The lemon and mint lifts the whole thing. This is lovely served either warm or at room temperature. A Greek-style salad with some tomatoes, feta cheese, and red onion would work perfectly as an accompaniment.

If using acorn or other small summer squash, just cut off a thin slice from the base so that they stand upright without wobbling, then cut off a lid and scoop out the seeds to make a cavity. If using zucchini, halve them lengthwise and, using a teaspoon, remove the seeds in the center to leave a "boat" shape. Season the cut surfaces with salt and leave them upside-down to drain. In two separate bowls, cover the capers and currants with warm water and leave them to soak.

When the squashes or zucchini have drained for 45–60 minutes, rinse them, pat dry, then steam for 10–12 minutes until just tender. Drain well on paper towels. Preheat the oven to 375°F.

Meanwhile, gently sauté the onion in 2 tablespoons of the oil with a pinch of salt until soft and sweet, about 10–15 minutes. Add the garlic and cook for another 3–4 minutes. Drain the capers and currants. Mix the onion and garlic with all the other ingredients except the egg, remaining oil, and lemon juice. Season to taste. Stir in the egg for a firmer stuffing, if desired. Put the squash or zucchini in a baking dish and fill the cavities with the stuffing. Mix together the remaining oil and lemon juice and spoon it over the vegetables. Bake in the preheated oven for 30–35 minutes, basting once, until golden and crisp on top. Serve warm with a Greek-style salad.

sweet things and preserves

spiced pumpkin & apple pie

for the pastry

1½ cups all-purpose flour

6½ tablespoons unsalted butter, chilled

3 tablespoons confectioners' sugar

1 egg yolk

1 teaspoon grated orange zest

for the filling

1 lb. prepared pumpkin, cut into chunks

5 tablespoons lightly salted butter

½ cup light brown or white sugar

2 tablespoons honey

3 eggs, beaten

½ teaspoon each ground cinnamon, ground ginger, and freshly grated nutmeg

finely grated zest and juice of 1 unwaxed lemon

1 large tart apple (such as Granny Smith), peeled, cored, and coarsely grated

confectioners' sugar, to dust

heavy cream, chilled, to serve

a deep, 9–10-inch diameter, metal pie plate

Serves 8–10

This is not, I grant you, the usual pumpkin pie. But much as I love the traditional version, I wanted to try something that had a lighter, slightly sharper flavor and adding a tart apple did the trick.

Put the flour, butter, and confectioners' sugar in a food processor with a pinch of salt and whizz until the mixture resembles breadcrumbs. Add the egg yolk, orange zest, and 2 tablespoons ice water and whizz again until the dough forms a ball. Turn onto a work surface and form into a smooth ball, wrap in foil and chill in the fridge for 1 hour.

Preheat the oven to 375°F. Roll out the pastry to line the pie plate. Support the sides with foil, prick the base, then bake blind in the preheated oven for 10 minutes. Remove the foil and bake again until just light brown. Remove from the oven and reduce the heat to 350°F.

Meanwhile, steam the pumpkin until tender. Purée it, then let it drip in a non-reactive sieve for 30 minutes or longer. You should have about 1¼ cups purée. Melt the butter, sugar, and syrup together, then beat into the pumpkin purée with the eggs, spices, lemon zest, and juice and apple. Pour the filling into the part-baked pie crust.

Roll out any pastry trimmings to make a decorative top. Put the pie on a baking sheet and bake in the preheated oven for about 40–50 minutes until the filling is firm and cooked through (protect the pastry edges with foil if they seem to be cooking too much). Dust with confectioners' sugar and serve warm, rather than hot, with chilled heavy cream.

sweet squash, pecan, & maple syrup tart

for the pastry

1⅓ cups all-purpose flour

2 tablespoons confectioners' sugar

6 tablespoons unsalted butter, chilled

1 egg yolk

1–2 tablespoons freshly squeezed lemon juice

for the filling

2 tablespoons unsalted butter

10 oz. prepared squash or pumpkin, coarsely grated

¼ cup raw sugar

2 tablespoons bourbon or rum

⅔ cup pecan halves, half of them chopped

2 eggs

grated zest of 1 unwaxed lemon

⅔ cup dark, pure maple syrup

½ teaspoon pure vanilla extract

⅔ cup heavy cream

confectioners' sugar, to dust

a deep, 8–9 inch diameter, metal tart pan with removable bottom

Serves 8

I imagined this tart long before I made it, and it happens to be one of those rare recipes that tastes just as good, if not better, in reality than on the mind's palate. The squash cuts the rich toffee of the more traditional pecan pie making it softer and more tender. The maple syrup adds a subtle smokiness. You'll need a sweet, orange-fleshed squash or pumpkin here; any of the French or Italian varieties (such as Jaspée de Vendée, Sucrine du Berry, or Pleine de Naples) will work, as will Delicata squash. It's best served warm, not hot, with chilled cream or vanilla ice cream.

To make the pastry, put the flour, confectioners' sugar, and butter in a food processor and whizz until the mixture resembles coarse breadcrumbs. Add the egg yolk and sufficient lemon juice, a little at a time, to make a ball of dough. Wrap in foil and chill in the fridge for 45 minutes. Roll the dough out on a floured work surface and line the tart pan. Chill for a further 30 minutes. Preheat the oven to 375°F. Support the sides of the tart with foil and bake in the preheated oven for 12 minutes. Remove the foil, press down any air bubbles in the base and bake for another 10 minutes or until pale brown. Remove from the oven and reduce the heat to 350°F.

Meanwhile, melt the butter in a skillet and gently sauté the squash for about 5 minutes until tender and lightly browned. Increase the heat a little, add 2 tablespoons of the raw sugar and cook until it caramelizes and melts around the squash. Add the bourbon and cook briskly until a sticky syrup forms, then mix in the chopped pecans. Spoon the squash mixture into the tart crust and arrange the pecan halves on top. Beat together the eggs, remaining sugar, lemon zest, maple syrup, and vanilla extract, then gradually beat in the cream. Pour the mixture into the tart crust. Bake in the still-hot oven for about 35–40 minutes, until puffed up and the center retains a very slight wobble.

zucchini, lemon, & poppyseed cake with lemon butter frosting

3 tablespoons poppyseeds

finely grated zest of 2 unwaxed lemons

⅓ cup milk

2 sticks unsalted butter, softened

1⅓ cups packed brown sugar

4 large eggs, separated

½ teaspoon pure vanilla extract

1½ cups self-rising flour, sifted

⅔ cup almonds, blanched and ground

8 oz. zucchini, trimmed and coarsely grated

½ teaspoon cream of tartar

for the frosting

1 cup confectioner's sugar

2 tablespoons butter, melted

2–3 tablespoons freshly squeezed lemon juice

1 teaspoon finely grated lemon zest

a 9–10-inch diameter, round cake pan, buttered and lined

Serves 8–10

There is a lovely retro charm, redolent of 1950s cookbooks, about making a sweet cake with a vegetable that's usually served savory. Of course, the zucchini here performs the same function as grated carrot does in the more familiar carrot cake. It keeps this cake wonderfully fresh and moist.

Preheat the oven to 375°F. Put the poppyseeds and lemon zest in a small bowl. Heat the milk until hot, stir it into the poppyseed mixture, and let it cool while you make the cake mixture.

Cream the butter and sugar together until very light and fluffy. Beat in the egg yolks, one at a time, followed by the vanilla extract, flour, and almonds. Fold in the zucchini followed by the poppyseed mixture. In a separate, grease-free bowl, whisk the eggs whites with the cream of tartar until stiff, then fold the egg whites into the cake mixture. Scrape the mixture into the prepared pan, smooth down and bake in the center of the preheated oven for 50–60 minutes until the cake is just firm to the touch and a skewer inserted into the center comes out clean with no uncooked mixture sticking to it. Let the cake cool in the pan for 10 minutes before turning onto a wire rack.

When cool, sift the confectioners' sugar into a bowl, make a well in the center and add the still-hot melted butter. Start to mix, adding sufficient lemon juice, a little at a time, to make a spreadable frosting. Mix in the lemon zest, then spread over the cake. Leave for 1–2 hours to set before serving.

zucchini & ricotta loaf

6½ oz. zucchini, trimmed and coarsely grated

3¼ cups bread flour, plus a little extra as necessary

¾ cup organic kamut (see page 23) or spelt flour

1¼ teaspoons salt

1½ teaspoons fast-action dry yeast

2–3 tablespoons chopped herbs of your choice (see right)

½ teaspoon sugar

4 oz. ricotta or sieved cottage cheese, well-drained in a sieve

1 cup freshly grated Parmesan cheese

¾ cup warm water

1 tablespoon olive oil

sea salt

Makes 1 large loaf

Adding grated zucchini and ricotta to this loaf makes it extra light and moist with a good chewy texture. You can vary the herbs according to taste, but parsley, chervil, and maybe a little tarragon or dill (the mixture the French call *fines herbes*) is a good place to start. It is a delicious bread to serve with smoked salmon, and it is also good grilled and served as an accompaniment to a bowl of soup, as grilling brings out the taste of the cheese.

Put the grated zucchini in a bowl and toss with 1 teaspoon salt. Put in a colander to drain for about 30–40 minutes, then squeeze out the excess water with your hands. Put the flours in a large bowl and add the salt and yeast. Stir in the herbs and zucchini.

Dissolve the sugar in the warm water, then add to the flour mixture with the drained cheese, Parmesan, and the oil. Start to bring together to form a dough. You might need a little extra flour to stop it being too sticky, but do not add too much. Cover and let it rest for 10 minutes, then turn it out onto a lightly floured surface and knead for 5 minutes until smooth and elastic. (As you knead, the dough will get stickier as the zucchini give up their moisture, so add a dusting of flour, but again, not too much.) Put it into the lightly oiled bowl, cover and let it rise at warm room temperature (not too hot) for about 90 minutes until doubled in size. Then punch down to deflate, knead gently for a few seconds, then cover again and let it rise for about 40 minutes.

Turn the dough onto a work surface, knead to deflate, then shape into a round and score the top in a criss-cross pattern with a sharp knife. Put on a large, floured baking sheet, cover and let it rise in a warm, not hot, place for 30–40 minutes. Meanwhile, preheat the oven to 425°F. Dust the top of the loaf with some extra flour, then bake in the preheated oven for about 40 minutes until the loaf sounds hollow when tapped on the base. Cool on a wire rack before serving.

squash & eggplant chutney

2 lbs. prepared orange-fleshed squash or pumpkin, diced

2 large eggplants, diced

1½ lbs. onions, chopped

4 garlic cloves, crushed

2–3 red chiles, seeded and finely sliced or chopped (leave the seeds in if you want heat)

1 tablespoon each crushed coriander seeds and brown mustard seeds

finely shredded zest and juice of 1 unwaxed orange

2-oz piece of fresh ginger

1¾ cups cider vinegar or white wine vinegar

2 cups sugar, warmed

2 teaspoons salt, plus extra to taste

cayenne or dried hot pepper flakes, to taste

a small piece of cheesecloth

kitchen string

4–5 sterilized preserving jars with new lids and screwbands (see note on page 4)

Makes 4–5 medium (12 oz.) jars

This is a golden chutney flecked with the dark purple of the eggplant and the red of the chile peppers. I make it with white sugar to preserve the glorious autumnal colors of the squash or pumpkin, but you could use brown sugar if you prefer a deeper color and flavor. Serve it with bread and cheese, with ham and cured meats, or spread thickly to spice up any sandwich. It will keep for at least 12 months in a dark, cool place. Keep in the fridge once opened.

Put the squash and eggplant in a large, stainless steel saucepan with the onions, garlic, chiles, crushed coriander and mustard, and the orange zest and juice. Bash the ginger with a rolling pin to bruise it, tie it in a piece of cheesecloth and bury it in the mixture. Pour over the vinegar. Bring to a boil, then simmer very gently, part-covered, for 40–50 minutes until the squash is fully tender. Stir in the warmed sugar and the salt, stir until the sugar dissolves, then bring to a boil and cook briskly, stirring every few minutes, until the mixture is thick and the liquid almost all absorbed, about 30–40 minutes. Stir very frequently towards the end of cooking to prevent the mixture from sticking to the base of the pan.

It is ready when a wooden spoon drawn over the base of the pan leaves a clear channel for a few seconds. Adjust the seasoning to taste with salt and cayenne. Discard the ginger, and then spoon the hot chutney straight into dry sterilized jars. Seal immediately, then invert. Let cool before turning the right way up. Store for at least 4 weeks before using.

pumpkin & ginger jam

Dorothy Jones.

2¼ lbs. prepared pumpkin, diced

grated zest and juice of 2 large unwaxed lemons

5 cups granulated sugar

3-inch piece of fresh ginger, sliced

1 lb. tart apples, peeled, cored, and chopped

2–3 oz. stem ginger in syrup, drained and cut into shreds

a small piece of cheesecloth

kitchen string

4–5 sterilized preserving jars with new lids and screwbands (see note on page 4)

Makes 4–5 small (8 oz.) jars

Pumpkin makes an unexpectedly fragrant and gloriously amber-colored preserve. Serve this jam as a filling for cakes or tarts or with your toast or croissant at breakfast. You could use any variety of pumpkin sold in Caribbean and Greek food stores—avoid the very savory squash such as Butternut or Red Onion. This recipe makes a softly set jam, which will store well for at least 9 months, but keep in the fridge once opened.

In a large non-reactive bowl, layer the pumpkin, lemon zest, and sugar. Wrap the fresh ginger and any lemon pips and flesh in a piece of cheesecloth tied with string and bury it in the middle of the pumpkin. Pour over the lemon juice, cover with plastic wrap, and leave in a cool place for 24 hours, stirring once.

Pour the mixture into a large preserving pan and add the apples. Tie the bag of ginger and lemon mixture to the handle of the pan so that the bag is suspended in the mixture.

Stir over low heat until the sugar completely dissolves, then increase the heat and simmer gently until the pumpkin softens. Increase the heat again and boil vigorously until setting point is reached, about 8–10 minutes*. Stir in the stem ginger. Remove the cheesecloth bag, squeezing it against the side of the pan, then stir in the stem ginger. Spoon the hot mixture into sterilized jars and seal immediately.

*To test for set. As the jam boils it will start to become thicker and more syrupy. Take it off the heat and put a teaspoonful on a saucer that you have chilled in the fridge. Leave for 5 minutes, then push the surface of the jam with your finger—if it wrinkles, the jam has reached setting point, otherwise boil again, testing at 4–5-minute intervals.

mail order and websites

WHERE TO BUY

Natural food stores and most supermarkets offer a wide range of summer and winter squashes plus pie pumpkins. Packages of peeled and seeded Butternut squash are now standard nearly everywhere. We suggest exploring farmers' markets and roadside farm stands for the more unusual varieties.

www.localharvest.org
An invaluable resource for finding locally grown organic foods. The site lists farmers' markets, family farms, and other sources of sustainably grown food in your region, as well as links to restaurants and like-minded stores.

www.ams.usda.gov/ farmersmarkets
Tel: 1-800-384-8704
According to the USDA's Farmers' Market Directory, there are now nearly 4,500 farmers' markets operating in the United States—more than twice the number of ten years ago. Check the website or dial the hotline to locate the farmers' market closest to you.

GROW YOUR OWN

Many pumpkin and squash devotees grow their own favorite varieties. Good sources for heirloom and hard-to-find seeds include:

Baker Creek Heirloom Seeds
www.rareseeds.com
Located in the Ozarks near Mansfield, Missouri, Baker Creek works to preserve America's gardening heritage and offers more than 12,000 unique varieties of seeds, including well over 100 squashes and pumpkins, among them the Italian Marina di Chioggia, the French Jaspée de Vendée and Sucrine du Berry, plus Japanese Kabocha, Hokkaido and Black Futsu.

Seed Savers Exchange
www.seedsavers.org
Tel: 563-382-5990
This nonprofit organization in Iowa is attempting to save the world's diverse garden heritage for future generations by building a network of people committed to collecting, conserving and sharing heirloom seeds and plants. Among their extensive squash collection you'll find the strange and beautiful Galeux d'Eysines and the Lady Godiva, grown for its hull-less seeds. You can order seeds directly from their website.

www.italianseedandtool.com
Tel: 575-398-6111
Tatum, New Mexico is home to Italian Seed and Tool, the source for Italian seeds for Italian vegetables. The zucchini section alone is worth a visit to the website. The firm also sells a range of fine Italian garden and kitchen tools.

Kitazawa Seed Company
www.kitazawa.seed.com
Tel: 510-595-1188
Kitazawa Seed Company is the oldest seed company in America specializing in Asian vegetable seeds. The California company offers an extensive selection of Japanese squash seeds including Blue Kuri, Red Skin Kabocha, and Akehima, a baby Kabocha.

Gardeners' Supply Company
www.gardenerssupply.com
Tel: 1-888-833-1412,
Visit their store and display garden at:
180 Intervale Road,
Burlington
Vermont 05401

This innovative firm has a number of raised bed options, trellises, and large, self-watering planters for novice and experienced vegetable gardeners.

SPECIALTY INGREDIENTS

A number of recipes in this book call for specialty ingredients which might not be available in your local store. We recommend the following online sources and stores:

www.tienda.com
Spanish ingredients available to buy on-line, such as pimentón (Spanish smoked paprika), chorizo, and fine olive oils.

www.zamourispices.com
Moroccan ingredients available to buy online such as preserved lemons, Moroccan spices, and olive oils.

www.penzeys.com
Top quality herbs and spices including saffron, ground sumac, and chiles available to buy online. See website for details of retail stores throughout the United States.

www.wholefoodsmarket.com
Whole Foods Market is the world's largest retailer of natural and organic foods, with more than 140 stores across the United States and Canada.

index

conversion chart

Weights and measures have been rounded up or down to make measuring easier.

Volume equivalents:

American	Metric	Imperial
1 teaspoon	5 ml	
1 tablespoon	15 ml	
¼ cup	60 ml	2 fl.oz.
⅓ cup	75 ml	2½ fl.oz.
½ cup	125 ml	4 fl.oz.
⅔ cup	150 ml	5 fl.oz. (¼ pint)
¾ cup	175 ml	6 fl.oz.
1 cup	250 ml	8 fl.oz.

Weight equivalents:

Imperial	Metric
1 oz.	30 g
2 oz.	55 g
3 oz.	85 g
3½ oz.	100 g
4 oz.	115 g
5 oz.	140 g
6 oz.	175 g
8 oz. (½ lb.)	225 g
9 oz.	250 g
10 oz.	280 g
11½ oz.	325 g
12 oz.	350 g
13 oz.	375 g
14 oz.	400 g
15 oz.	425 g
16 oz. (1 lb.)	450 g

Measurements:

Inches	Cm
¼ inch	0.5 cm
½ inch	1 cm
¾ inch	1.5 cm
1 inch	2.5 cm
2 inches	5 cm
3 inches	7 cm
4 inches	10 cm
5 inches	12 cm
6 inches	15 cm
7 inches	18 cm
8 inches	20 cm
9 inches	23 cm
10 inches	25 cm
11 inches	28 cm
12 inches	30 cm